To Cody –
From
friends –
Lonnie E. Brown
Roberta Simpson Brown

Spooky, Kooky Poems for Kids

by

Lonnie E. Brown
and
Roberta Simpson Brown

PublishAmerica
Baltimore

First printing

All characters appearing in this work are fictitious. Any resemblance to real persons, living or dead, is purely coincidental.

ISBN: 1-4241-3940-6
PUBLISHED BY PUBLISHAMERICA, LLLP
www.publishamerica.com
Baltimore

Printed in the United States of America

Dedication

This book is dedicated to Lonnie's parents, Lena Mae Brown and the late Lucian E. Brown. It is also dedicated to all the kids we know. We are so lucky to have had all of you in our lives!

Acknowledgments from Lonnie

Thanks to my mom and dad, Lucian and Lena Brown,
who taught me their love of music and poetry.

Thanks to my brothers and sisters, Neline Kerr, Lewis Brown, Del
Vontrice Hurt, El Wanda Horsley, and H. L. (Charlie) Brown, and
their families for their support and encouragement.

Acknowledgments from Roberta

Thanks to my parents, Tom and Lillian Simpson, and my sister,
Fatima Atchley, who taught me how much fun poetry is!

Thanks to my students through the years, who
taught me as much as I taught them!
Thanks to my friend Joseph Dubronski Jones,
poet, singer, and master artist who helped the students and me
experience the beauty of the arts!

And a special thanks to all our friends from childhood to now,
especially Robert Parker and all our ghost hunter friends, who make
life interesting, fun, and full of wonderful things to write about!

THE MONSTERS DID IT

"Your toys are scattered all over the floor!
You know I strictly forbid it!"
"It wasn't me, Mom," the little boy said.
"It was the monsters that did it!"

"Where is my pen?" the father asked.
"Have you taken it somewhere and hid it?"
"I didn't move it anywhere, Dad.
It was the monsters that did it."

"What are we going to do with this boy?"
The father and mother sighed.
"He's done some naughty things before,
But this is the first time he's lied."

The parents went up to their little boy's room
And turned the night light on.
The room was empty and damp and cold.
The little boy was gone!

A tied-up package was on the bed.
They picked it up and undid it.
All that fell out were bloody bones
And a note: *The monsters did it.*

BARK! BARK!

(For Howard, Patrick, Zeke, Lily, Tuff, Inky,
and all the other dogs I love!)

Bark! Bark!
That's the dog next door.
Bark! Bark!
What are you barking for?
Bark! Bark!
Do you want some chow?
Bark! Bark!
You can stop it now!
Bark! Bark!
Do I hear a creak?
Someone's out there, trying to sneak!
Bark! Bark!
I'm dialing 911.
The man's trying to get my lock undone!
Bark! Bark!
The man pays no heed
To the barking dog that's got him treed!
Bark! Bark!
Police sirens wail.
They cuff that man and take him to jail!
Bark! Bark!
Now I sleep like a log
'Cause I'm protected by the barking dog!
Bark! Bark!
Bark! Bark!
Bark! Bark!

THE GOBLIN

A goblin is hiding back under my bed.
He's just like the one in the story I read.
He has a wide mouth and a big yellow head,
And I think he's hungry and wants to be fed.

The first time I knew that he was about,
I'd turned back the covers to put my feet out.
I just caught a glimpse, but I have no doubt
He'll gobble me whole if I get up or shout.

I have no choice but to lie here and wait.
If Mom would come up, it would really be great!
I hope she gets here before it's too late.
I don't want to end up on that goblin's plate.

I hear a noise, so I will be quiet.
Maybe the goblin will sleep through the night.
Here under my covers, I'll be out of sight
Until Mom comes up and turns on the light.

She's in my room now and I feel much better.
I hope the goblin won't reach out and get her,
Like the story I read with the babysitter.
Mom wants to check, so I guess I'll let her.

She's poking under the bed with my bat
At the very spot the monster is at!
She says all that's there is my old fishing hat.
But the goblin *was* real! I'm quite sure of that!

THE TROUBLE WITH SANTA

The chubby old fellow
Walked into the house,
Sank in his chair
And sighed to his spouse.

"Bring me some water
And give me my pill!
I've had a hard time
Spreading cheer and goodwill."

"My dear," she asked him
With wifely insight
As she patted his shoulder,
"Did you have a hard night?"

"Hard night?" he sputtered.
"If only you knew!
You just can't imagine
What all I've been through!

"First I loaded the sleigh,
And then, very blunt,
Rudolph announced
He would *not* be in front.

" 'But Rudolph," I reasoned,
'It's foggy tonight.
I can't get along
If I don't have a light.'

"Well, after much coaxing,
He took his position
And so off we went
On our annual mission.

"We flew over country
And city and town.
The sleigh dipped and swayed
As we went up and down.

"I struggled down chimneys,
Both narrow and wide.
And I'd fall in the fireplace
Or get stuck inside.

"How I lived through it
The Lord only knows."
But all his wife said was,
"Nick, look at your clothes!"

But Nick just ignored
Her wifely protest
And went right on talking
And told her the rest.

"I've given out presents
Of all shapes and sizes
For millions and millions
Of Christmas surprises.

"Here I go flying
All over the map
And ungrateful kids
Set me some kind of trap.

"And they ask silly questions
'Til I'd pop my cork!
"Like 'Is your tummy jelly?'
Or 'Are you a stork?'

"If it wasn't enough
To face those little fiends,
I kept getting picked up
On darn radar screens!"

"You must watch your language,"
His wife put in quick.
"You must mind your manners,
For you are Saint Nick!"

"Manners, the Devil!"
Nick managed to wheeze.
"Starting right now,
I will do as I please!

"I'm tired of pretending
I'm something I ain't!
And just after Christmas,
I sure ain't no saint!"

COSTUME PARTY

It's a costume party!
What shall I wear?
A witch's dress
And long, black hair?
A Santa suit
With a soft, white beard?
Would an Easter Bunny outfit
Look too weird?
I could glue on black feathers
And go as a crow,
Or dress like a farmer
And carry a hoe!
I think I'll do what
I'd really enjoy.
I'll cover my fangs,
And go as a boy!

TRUTH AND CONSEQUENCES

There was a handsome young gent,
Who always said what he meant.
He said to a miss
That he'd like a kiss.
Now his head has a dent!

FIRE STARTER

Daniel played with matches
And defective Christmas lights.
He left lint in the dryer
When he dried his clothes at night.

He laughed at all the safety rules
To help prevent a fire.
Once he went out in a storm
And touched a downed *live wire!*

Daniel knows the rules now.
Why, he could teach some classes!
But it doesn't do him any good,
'Cause he's a pile of ashes!

SUBSTITUTE

School was in session
And we had a sub.
We students were members
Of the *Let's Get Her Club*!

While she wrote on the board,
I sneaked to her chair
And quietly left
A surprise for her there.

When she turned and saw it,
She let out a yell.
"Which one of you did this?"
But no one would tell.

"What's the big deal?" we asked.
"It's only a snake!
It's not even real!
It's just a big fake!"

She glared as fierce
As I've ever seen,
And said to the class,
"I think you're all mean!

"If you won't say who did it,
I won't go on guessin'.
But I think it's time
That I taught you a lesson!"

Then in a twinkle,
She started to change!
Her skin got all scaly!
She really looked strange!

We watched in amazement
As off came her skin,
And another one grew
Where the old one had been!

We jumped up screaming
And ran for the door
While our teacher slithered
Around on the floor!

Then something stopped us
Right there in the hall.
We heard the voice
Of the principal call!

"Where are you going?
Now get back inside!"
"We can't! There's a monster!"
We students replied.

He went to the doorway
And looked in the aisle.
Then he turned back
With a cold, wicked smile.

"Go to your seats now
And stay 'til the break.
It's not a big deal, kids!
It's only a snake!"

EXCUSES, EXCUSES

Two middle school students were late.
They told their teacher to wait.
They had to confer
Before they told her
The stories they had to get straight.

BOGEY MAN

The Bogey Man was outside
Sitting in a tree.
I looked at him
And he looked at me!

He crawled among the leaves
And hid on the branches.
I closed my window.
No use in taking chances.

I don't know how he got there
Or why he chose this place,
But during a thunderstorm,
I thought I saw his face.

His eyes were bright and shiny.
His fur was sleek and wet.
He made a dreadful squalling sound
I never will forget.

I hurried to my father's room
And told him what I heard.
He walked down the hall with me
And never said a word.

He took a big flashlight
And shined it in the dark.
This woke our dog up,
And he began to bark.

The neighbors yelled and shouted
That we should all be quiet.
I guess all the commotion
Gave the Bogey Man a fright.

For when Dad climbed up the tree
Where I had seen him sittin',
He found that the Bogey Man
Had turned into a kitten!

UNDER THE LAKE

There's a dark cave under the lake,
And a big slimy thing lives in it.
If you dive into the lake to swim,
It will gobble you up in a minute!

If you should sit on the bank to fish,
Keep your toes out of the water!
I know a girl who dangled her feet
And the slimy thing came up and caught her!

Don't go out in boats, and don't water ski!
You can't come out a winner!
How do I know the thing is real?
It ate me last night for dinner!

TORTURE

You can lock me in a closet
That's small and dark.
You can throw me in the ocean
With a hungry shark.
You can send me to my room
Until I grow old.
You can me feed me bread
Covered up with mold.
You can make me go barefoot,
And walk on nails.
When you hear a train coming,
You can tie me to the rails.
But all of your tortures
And all of your shouts,
Will never make me eat
These *Brussels sprouts!*

WHY

Why can't I play baseball?
I can run and slide!
Why can't I play hide-and-seek?
I know how to hide.
Why can't I play basketball?
I can pounce on balls.
Why can't I play football?
I'm never hurt in falls.
It seems like I miss all the fun
Wherever I am at.
I'm not allowed to join in games
'Cause I'm a kitty cat!

LILY

My friend's dog Lily
Was white as snow.
Peopled *oohed* and *aahed*
Wherever she'd go.

If they approached her
She'd change their tune,
And they wouldn't be
Coming back very soon.

That sweet little face
Would snarl and scowl.
And then she'd let out
This awful growl.

One time when
I didn't retreat,
She nipped the toes
On both my feet!

In her territory,
She followed rules,
But she got kicked out
Of obedience schools!

She was the only dog
I couldn't win,
And I didn't want
Ever to see her again!

Then one day,
God called her home.
My greatest adversary
Was gone!

She treated me bad,
And I know it's silly,
But every now and then,
I miss old Lily!

CURED

My sister says she's sick
Mom does not believe her.
She doesn't have a cough.
She doesn't have a fever.
She says it's a stomachache,
But Mom knows it will pass
As soon as she misses
Her P. E. class!

LOCKED OUT

I'm surrounded by darkness
And I'm locked outside!
Every door, every window,
I've tried and I've tried!
But it is so hopeless.
I can't get inside.

I do have my key,
But it won't turn the lock.
Everyone's sleeping,
So I don't want to knock.
It's midnight, I know,
From the chimes of the clock.

I move to the streetlight
Where I stood before,
And look at the numbers
And read them once more.
Gee! I'm so embarrassed!
I'm at the wrong door!

SPIDER

A spider! A spider!
It's right beside her!
She doesn't know it wants to be her friend.

A spider! A spider!
Now it can't abide her.
She got the bug spray and did it in!

SOAP OPERA

My father sang in the shower.
He did it hour after hour.
We gave him a quarter
To turn off the water
Because the notes were all sour!

THE WITHERED HAND

The old man with the withered hand
Delivered papers on our street.
He always smiled, so I smiled back.
He was someone nice to greet.

I gave him a cup of hot chocolate once
When it was very cold.
I noticed it was a difficult thing
For the withered hand to hold.

Some of the kids would laugh at him
And make signs like a claw.
But he ignored the things they did
Just like he never saw.

The last time I saw him,
I didn't know it was the end.
He said to me, "I thank you.
You've been a fine young friend."

Someone else took on his route,
And then one day I read
In the paper that he used to bring
That the poor old man was dead.

The paper brought us other news.
A killer was on a spree.
He'd murdered several people.
One lived close to me.

We locked our doors and windows
And stayed inside at night.
But one night I woke up.
The moon was shining bright.

First I saw a shadow.
Then I saw a knife.
Then I saw the killer
Who had come to take my life.

But something came between us!
It held the man in check!
*Then I saw the withered hand
Pressing on his neck!*

GHOST TRAIN

Clickety-Clack! Clickety-Clack!
Midnight Flyer is coming down the track!
Tracks are blocked, the signal fails.
The *Midnight Flyer* jumps the rails.
Screams and moans fill the air.
The hurt and dying are everywhere.

Clickety-Clack! Clickety-Clack!
Every anniversary, the train comes back!
It takes somebody else to join the dead.
This year's anniversary is just ahead!

Clickety-Clack! Clickety-Clack!
Listen to the ghost train coming down the track!
If you hear the whistle, you'd better run and hide!
Ghost train's a-comin'!
Gonna take you for a ride!

Clickety-Clack! Clickety-Clack! Clickety-Clack!

GO FIGURE

Why does the math teacher
Call on me?
I sit in the back,
But she can see.

Every day this week
She sat and stared
And seemed to know
I was unprepared!

She called my name
To solve the problem.
I stood at the board,
And my knees were wobblin'.

I tried and tried,
But I took too long.
Every answer I got
Was wrong!

Finally she sent me
Back to my seat.
This was one mistake
I would not repeat!

Today I have
All my homework done!
She can call on me
For every one!

I raised my hand
To show what I did,
But today she called
On another kid!

THE HOUSE NEXT DOOR

When I looked at the house next door,
I was absolutely certain
I saw a shadowy form reach up
And slowly move a curtain.

I felt something watching me!
It made me feel so creepy,
I jumped in bed and covered up
Until I got real sleepy!

I woke up later in the night
And looked at the house next door.
A small light floated on the wall
And then I saw no more.

I know that something's over there
And that it's trying to tempt me.
But I'm not going near the place!
The house next door is *empty!*

FOG

They came last night
In a heavy fog.
I knew by the whimpering
Of my dog.

I felt them staring!
It was so intense!
My dad tells me
It makes no sense.

But I know what I know
And I see what I see!
The ghosts in the fog
Are coming for me!

I begin screaming
As they fly through the air!
Then Dad wakes me up
From another nightmare.

FIRED UP

I want to be a firefighter!
I want to start right now!
I'm going to the station
To see if they'll teach me how.

I want to ride the engine
As it streaks off down the street.
I want to be a hero
To everyone I meet!

I want to climb the ladder
And rescue kids and pets
And older folks who can't escape
The worse the fire gets!

I'll help the firemen hold the hose
And spray on walls of flames.
I'll talk to news reporters
Who'll mention all our names.

So when can I get started?
I know this is my fate.
Firemen have such glamorous lives!
I can hardly wait!

Oh, you want me to clear the bay?
And help you mop the floors?
And cook and get equipment out
And do these other chores?

I don't want to check fire hydrants!
Don't want to check the hose,
Or do the drills, or wash the trucks.
Or wear such heavy clothes!

I guess I'm having second thoughts.
Don't think I'm a jerk,
But I should never have gotten all fired up
Before I knew it was work!

THE SHIFTS OF TIME AND FATE

Through the shadows of the twilight,
Onward all the wagons pressed,
Trying hard to cross the mountains
As they pushed on farther west.

Over slopes, all steep and rocky,
Horses strained with all their might.
Drivers urged them toward the valley
Where they planned to camp that night.

Slowly all the wagons circled.
Very soon the campfire's gleam
Danced upon the sparkling water
Of a bubbling mountain stream.

Darkness fell and from a distance
Came a lonesome coyote's wail
Answered only by the bacon,
Sizzling, frying on the trail.

All had gather around the campfire
Where they sang a happy song.
"Sleep now," said the wagon master.
"We move out at crack of dawn."

Silence settled over the wagons.
In the darkness, deep and still,
Lay a girl whose mind kept wondering
What could lie beyond the hill.

She sat upright in the wagon
As she quickly looked about.
All was quiet; all were sleeping.
She climbed down and hurried out.

Something seemed to pull her onward,
An urge that could not be denied.
She slipped through the circled wagons
To the place her horse was tied.

Not a murmur did she utter
While the horse's steady stride
Brought her near the looming hillside
Where she longed so much to ride.

Back at camp amid the darkness
Moved two figures, in and out.
It was the sturdy wagon master,
And a tall, young Indian scout.

"Indian signs," the scout confided,
"I have seen them all along."
The wagon master quietly answered.
"They will not attack 'til dawn."

Far above the stars were twinkling.
Tension filled the air with vibes.
Both men knew the hills beyond them,
Were the homes of Indian tribes.

Thus the two men watched in silence
As the lonely night dragged on,
'Til the shouting broke the stillness,
"Help! Come quick! Miss Janie's gone!"

Figures darted about the wagons
Until a thorough search was made.
All the people prayed and waited,
  Trying not to be afraid.

Meanwhile Janie's horse sped onward.
Many knew that she had come.
And the news of her arrival
Was sent out by beating drums.

Other hoof beats then were throbbing,
Rushing toward her on the ground;
A snow-white horse, a dark-skinned rider
In a buckskin suit of brown.

Haunting eyes smiled at the maiden,
But his full lips never moved.
The blood within her veins was pounding.
Her restless heart, at last, was soothed!

Back at camp the search continued
Through the hills where she had roamed.
The wagon train would not be leaving
Until the hills had all been combed.

Each day at the dawn they waited
For the attack that did not come.
No one saw the lovely maiden.
No one heard a single drum.

Finally they could wait no longer.
There came the wagon master's shout,
"Wagons, ho!" The wheels were rolling.
The wagon train was pulling out.

Later, other settlers following
Through this rugged western land,
Said they saw a lovely maiden
Riding with an Indian band.

Riding on with reckless daring,
Never slowing down to wait,
She was doomed to ride forever
By the shifts of time and fate!

FOOD

What foods are your favorites?
What I like the most
Are fried eggs for breakfast
With butter on toast.

By lunch I am ready
For grilled cheese and soup,
With chocolate ice cream
(A really big scoop)!

By dinner I'm open
To fulfill my wishes
For veggies and salads
And all kinds of dishes.

Green beans and potatoes,
Rice and green peas,
Broccoli and boiled eggs,
Macaroni and cheese!

Wait! Stop here!
Excuse me a minute!
My stomach is empty!
It needs something in it!

THE ALARM

The men at Station 51
Were working hard one day
When they saw a little boy
Walk just inside the bay.

"My name is Joe Johnson,"
He told them with a smile.
"Dad's laid off, so is it okay
To shine shoes here for awhile?"

They all became his customers.
His business did quite well.
He spoke about his family,
And a homeless friend named Mel.

Time went by and then one day
At Station 51,
The firemen were surprised
When Joe didn't come.

They thought his dad went back to work,
And Joe got a vacation
From shining shoes for all the guys
That worked there at the station.

They all missed Joe very much
And were sorry he was gone,
But the men of Station 51
Had work to focus on.

One morning, they were all amazed
To see young Joe was back.
"Come help my friend!" he pleaded.
"Mel's trapped in a shack!"

"It's right there by the pier," he said.
"Hurry if you can!
He's going to die if you don't come!"
Then the boy turned and ran.

The captain sent an engine crew
To check the story out.
Mel was trapped just as Joe said
And flames were all about.

As the paramedics treated Mel
They asked if he knew Joe.
"He came and sounded the alarm
And told us where to go."

""Yes," said Mel, "I knew him!
But it couldn't have been Joe.
He was struck and killed by a city bus
About six weeks ago."

NO SUCH THING AS A WITCH

There is no such thing as a witch,
But I wonder about Miss Rose!
She keeps a broom in the corner
And she has a very long nose!

There is no such thing as a witch,
But in class when Miss Rose yells
And stirs her strong black coffee,
I think she's casting spells.

Charlie Casey *did* get sick.
And Nancy didn't pass!
And all of this happened
After they'd been bad in class.

There is no such thing as a witch,
But it makes me question
Why Billy threw spit balls in class
And then got indigestion!

There is no such thing as a witch.
But what if that's not true?
I'm going to be good around Miss Rose.
Come on now! Wouldn't you?

SLEEPOVER CRASHER

I hear voices.
I hear screams.
I see curlers
And pimple creams.

I hear running
In the halls.
My sister and her friends
Are having a ball.

I smell popcorn
At two a.m.
They're telling ghost tales
With the lights on dim.

For a minute
I stand at the door,
And ask myself
What are brothers for!

I go to my room
And get a sheet.
I can't resist!
It's just too neat!

I moan while standing
By the door.
They grab their sleeping bags
From the floor.

They knock me down
As they run out!
The sleepover's over
For tonight, no doubt!

HEAD HUNTERS

When we go to visit
My Uncle Saul.
I see all the mounted heads
On his wall.

He says they're his trophies,
and that he likes to hunt.
I tell him I don't like it,
For I'm very blunt!

It makes me uneasy
When I look into their eyes.
"They can't hurt you,"
Uncle Saul replies.

It's not the heads that scare me.
It's something else I dread.
What if those headless bodies
Came hunting for their heads?

NIGHT THOUGHTS

Mom wakes me up.
A storm is coming fast.
We're going to the basement
Until it's passed.

We sit in the dark
For the power is out.
We can't see a thing
When we look about!

I sit here scared
In my pajamas!
That cold hand on mine
Had better be Momma's!

ANTIQUES

Dad bought an antique rocking chair
And put it in our den.
It's always rocking by itself
Whenever I walk in!

Yesterday I caught a glimpse
Of someone sitting there.
Her face was very wrinkled
And she had snow-white hair.

I really like the rocking chair,
But what I like the most
Is that we have, living in our house,
A very ancient ghost!

I think Dad got a bargain.
When all is said and done,
I think he purchased two antiques
Just for the price of one!

SOMETHING IN THE ATTIC

There is something in the attic,
And we can't sleep.
My sister says we should go
And take a peep!

But I can hear it walking.
It sounds big to me!
There's something in the attic
That I don't want to see!

There is something in the attic,
Walking across the floor.
It's coming down the stair steps.
It's right outside our door.

We hear heavy breathing.
We cover up our heads.
The door slowly opens.
We're shaking in our beds!

Then a weird laugh begins!
Another and another!
We beat the thing with our shoes.
It's just our stupid brother.

STORM DAMAGE

The storm blew strange things
Into our yard—
An empty brown bag,
A birthday card,

A book with wet pages,
An old magazine,
Some big, leafy branches,
And wire from a screen.

Dad gave me a garbage bag,
And, at his insistence,
I started picking up the mess—
But wait, in the distance…

A rumble of thunder!
A strong blast of wind!
I think a storm is headed
To our house again.

I'll wait to do all this work
For maybe today
The wind that first brought the mess
Will blow it all away!

REMOTE

Dad controls the TV
With his remote.
He switches the channels
Without our vote.
We don't like the programs
That he selects,
And what we want to see,
He rejects.

Mom let the problem
Go on for a while.
Then she came in
With a great big smile.
I knew as soon
As I saw her face
That Dad's remote control
Was in a remote place!

MODERN PUNISHMENT

I'm here in my room
Because I've been bad.
I yelled at my sister
And talked back to Dad.

My dad told me
To go straight to bed.
So I went to my room
And did what he said.

But I talked on my phone
And watched some TV.
I listened to music—
A brand new CD!

I was reading when Mom
Brought me cookies and stuff.
She said, "Punishment's over!
You've suffered enough!"

CLYDE

Clyde was a neighbor's boy
That people thought was tough.
He liked to fight and drink a lot
And generally live rough.

It's said he did some other things
That made his parents sad.
In any case, the folks back home
Were sure he'd turn out bad.

But people didn't take the time
To see his gentle side.
They wouldn't even listen
When I'd stick up for Clyde.

They never saw him give the love
That he had always lacked
To all the little weaker things
That others never backed.

They simply never would believe
Or try to understand
Why butterflies would fly to him
And light upon his hand.

When Clyde grew up, times were hard,
Job applicants were rejected.
So Clyde got money other ways
Just like most folks expected.

He served some time for forgery
And more for jumping bail,
And no one thought it sad that he
Should spend his life in jail.

I've watched the people shake their heads
And I've listened as they cussed him.
But I wonder if a man's all bad
If a butterfly can trust him.

ANIMAL KINGDOM

If our classroom had a name,
This is what it should be.
Animal Kingdom is perfect,
For this is what you'd see.

Freddy has a frog face
And always hops about.
Eddie is an elephant
Because he's big and stout.

Kristen waddles like a duck.
I swear I've heard her quack.
Priscilla is a parrot
Because she likes to yak.

Kathy is a kitty cat,
June Miller is a dog!
Harry's hungry all the time,
So we call him the Hog!

Betty's busy as a bee
Whenever flowers are bloomin'.
Too bad they all can't be like me!
I'm the perfect human!

GOOD LUNCH

Mom packed my lunch today
With healthy stuff as usual.
I had to take it with me
With no refusal!

In the cafeteria
I met my friends
And we all went
On an eating binge.

I traded peanut butter
For thick bologna,
And I traded my apple
For cheese and macaroni.

I exchanged my muffin
For a piece of chocolate cake
And never even thought
Of my sugar intake!

I drank a large Coke
Instead of milk,
And it all went down
Just as smooth as silk!

After school Mom asked,
"Did you like your lunch?"
"Sure did," I told her.
"Thanks a bunch!"

KU-COO

I'm pooped all the time.
I've got tired blood.
Mom says I wouldn't
Get well if I could.

But Mom's got asthma
And Daddy is sick.
My nephew's nose bleeds.
The dog has a tick.

My brother-in-law
Has a migraine headache.
And the veins in my poor
Old sister's legs break.

The plaster is busted.
The kitchen roof leaks.
The car won't run.
It just sits there and creaks.

We're all out of work
And our money is gone.
I guess the electricity
Will be turned off before long.

TV set's busted.
Toilet won't flush.
They're cutting the phone off
In a big rush!

Sis tries to tell us,
And we all just let her,
That things can't get worse,
So they've got to get better!

WELL, I COULD!

I can kill dragons.
I can eat fire!
I can walk without a net
On a high wire!
I can swim with sharks
And they won't get me!
Well, I *could*
If my mom would let me!

ODD EGG

I saw an egg
In a great big nest,
And something inside
Was trying its best
To crack the shell
And hatch right out.
When it did,
I began to shout!
"Who left this?
It's not funny!
Monsters don't come
From the Easter Bunny!"

SEEING IS BELIEVING

Randy saw a leprechaun.
Kevin saw a witch.
Chester saw a mermaid
Swimming in a ditch!
Susan saw a unicorn.
Julie saw an elf!
But I don't believe them
Unless I see them for myself!

GIFT TIME

I stayed home from school today
Because I had the flu.
People brought me gifts because
They thought that I'd feel blue.

Our neighbor brought me chocolate cake.
My little brother ate it!
I was too sick to keep it down
And he didn't want to waste it.

My friend brought me a new CD,
But my head hurt so bad
I couldn't listen to it,
So I gave it to my dad.

Mom's talking on my new cell phone
And I can't talk or yell.
Why can't I get gifts like this
Whenever I am well?

SUPERSTITIOUS

A small ghost follows me around,
But he is not malicious.
He likes to make fun of me
Because I'm superstitious!

I don't walk under ladders.
I always knock on wood.
I whistle passing graveyards,
Because it's understood

That you have to do these things
In order to survive!
So, Ghost, why are you laughing?
At least *I'm* still alive!

CLOSE CALL

When I walked home
From school today,
I passed the park
And stopped to play.

I knew I wasn't
Supposed to do it,
But they had a new swing
And I ran to it!

I hadn't swung
But a time or two
When a man showed up
Right out of the blue.

"I have a puppy
In my van!"
I jumped from the swing
And ran and ran.

Mom had warned me
Of the danger
Of this approach
By a total stranger.

When I got home,
I began to bawl
And told my parents
About my close call.

They called the police.
They caught the man!
I'll never go alone
To the park again!

GOLF

What if your dad
Gets mad playing golf?
Don't say he's angry.
Just say he's *teed off!*

DON'T RIDE WITH HIM

I knew I shouldn't ride with him,
But the school bus was late.
When he offered me a ride,
I didn't want to wait.

I knew I shouldn't ride with him.
Now I'm too scared to speak!
The thought of what could happen
Has me trembling and weak!

The tires screeched at the stop sign.
Then he zoomed ahead.
I'm praying when this ride ends,
I won't be hurt or dead!

I know I shouldn't ride with him!
My mom has warned me, but—
We got here safely, even though,
My dad drives like a nut!

WALKING SHOES

I bought the strangest pair of shoes
That walked all by themselves.
I guess they were made by leprechauns
Or maybe Santa's elves.

They moved my feet from place to place
When I just had a thought.
These strange shoes were comfortable,
The best I ever bought!

At first, I kept them cleaned and shined.
They walked about with pride.
But I got involved with other things
And let their grooming slide.

I guess they felt neglected.
Of course, I couldn't say.
Today when I went to put them on,
They had simply walked away.

QUICK CHANGE

I'm here at camp
And bored already.
The rain on my tent
Is loud and steady.

I guess I'm stuck here
For the night.
There are letters
I need to write.

Maybe my parents
Will come and get me.
I'd leave right now
If they'd just let me.

Out in the woods
I hear a noise!
It's the counselor
And the other boys.

How quickly things change!
I rush to get dressed.
I'd forgotten the night hike!
I'm no longer depressed.

HOUSE RULES

My parents bought a haunted house.
They really got it cheap.
We live with things that moan at night
And other things that creep.

We don't want to be
Ungracious hosts,
So we have house rules
For the ghosts.

Don't make the boards creak!
Don't make it cold.
Don't make fireballs
That smell like mold!

Don't pull our covers off!
Hold the criticism!
Follow the house rules
Or face an exorcism!

INTRUDER

Donnie's window was open,
And sometime in the night
Something floated through it
And gave him such a fright

That he threw back his covers
And streaked down the hall.
"Help me, Mom," he hollered
"It came right through the wall!"

"What are you talking about?"
His sleepy mom replied.
"The thing that came into my room!
It touched my neck and died!"

His mom went to check it out.
The time was very brief.
"Come see your intruder," she called.
And Donnie saw a leaf!

JUSTICE?

The boy stood by the haunted woods.
His mind was filled with doubt.
He'd heard that those who walked in these woods
Never, ever came out.

But this was the only shortcut,
And he had to go on home.
He couldn't go the usual way
Because the bridge was gone.

"I've been good," the boy said.
"I should have nothing to fear.
If there's any justice in the world,
I should come out of here."

He took a deep breath and stepped on the path
They called the haunted route.
I guess there is no justice!
The boy never came out.

RIDER

Sitting in the last row
Back on the bus
Is a little girl
Who is not like us.

She's very pale and silent.
Her clothes are out of style.
The few times I've seen her,
I've never seen her smile.

I described her to the driver,
Who sadly shook his head.
"It sounds like Maria,
The little girl that's dead.

She comes to warn others
Who are about to die.
They're the ones who see her.
I don't know why!"

DON'T TEMPT FATE

Don't laugh at fairies!
Don't sneer at ghosts
Or any apparition
That scares you most.

Don't grin at goblins
Or disrespect specters.
Don't make fun of monsters
Or creatures in lectures.

Don't tempt fate by jeering
Because I'll bet you,
As sure as you do,
They're going to come get you!

BATHROOM BEASTS

When Dad calls to me at night,
"It's your bath time, son!"
I always look around
To find a place to run.

What if alligators
Are hiding in the tub?
They could chomp my foot off
And leave a bloody stub.

What if a big old snake
Has slithered up the drain
And sinks its fangs into my leg
And causes awful pain?

My dad says if I am brave
And face the bathroom beasts,
That we'll put our pajamas on
And have a popcorn feast!

BACK TO SCHOOL

I hate going back to school!
I'm used to sleeping late.
I hate to stand at the bus stop
And wait and wait and wait.

I hate being herded along
To the cafeteria or gym
Until a teacher tells us
That we're to go with him.

I hate when teachers call the roll.
They never get names right.
I hate to go to the restrooms.
There's sure to be a fight.

My locker never opens.
The water fountains flood.
A kid squirts ink on my new white top.
The spot's as red as blood.

The teacher hands the schedules out
As we come through the door.
I take a seat by a handsome guy
I've never seen before.

He says our classes are the same.
His smile just makes me drool!
Now I'm thinking I am glad
That I am back in school.

OUT THERE

Moss-covered things rise up at night
And hide in my back yard.
They grab little kids with their mossy hands
If little kids let down their guard.

Headless ghosts and big black things
Come to my room sometimes.
They float on the walls and refuse to go
Until the hall clock chimes.

If you think that I'm not telling the truth,
Just look out your window tonight.
You'll see strange things move among the trees
That will make you shake with fright.

When I asked my dad what I could do
To keep these fiends away,
He said, "Point one of your shoes to the east,
And the other the other way."

When I asked my brother what he would suggest,
He said I should whisper perhaps
And that I should always cover my feet
When I lie down for naps.

My sister laughed when I asked her advice
And told me to skip the ice cream
That I eat every night before going to bed.
She thinks these are things that I dream.

You never know what is hiding out there
To creep up without any warning.
My mother assures me they'll all be gone
When the sun comes up in the morning!

CHILD'S WISH

I wish some ghouls would have a feast
   And invite my sitter, Miss Jones!
I wish she'd be their main course
   And that they'd crunch her bones.

   I wish they'd gobble all of her
      By the time they finish.
   Then she wouldn't be around
      To make me eat my spinach!

RECONSIDER

I always swim alone at night,
Especially after eating.
I walk in parks alone,
At risk to get a beating!

I eat all the foods
That are bad for me.
When there's lightning
I sit under a tree.

I ride my bike
without any lights,
And speed down slick roads
On rainy nights!

Did you say you'd like to be like me?
You must be some kidder!
I do these things because I'm dead!
You might want to reconsider!

EMPTY

There's an old empty house
Right down the street.
It's a spooky place
For kids to meet.

Our parents tell us
To stay outside.
There are too many dangers
Lurking inside.

Once we were playing
Right near the door,
When it began to thunder
And rain began to pour!

We pushed the door open
And ran in together
To keep ourselves dry
In the stormy weather.

Shadows moved
Along the walls
And lightning danced
In fiery balls!

There were moans and groans
And howls and wails,
And we remembered
The true ghost tales!

But we were brave!
We didn't run!
We stayed in the house
Until the storm was done.

We wanted to tell
How we'd faced the ghosts,
But the victory was empty.
We couldn't boast.

If our folks found out
We'd disobeyed,
They'd teach of the meaning
Of being afraid!

GETTING OLD!

It's my birthday.
I asked for a game.
Grandma sent her picture
In a big, gold frame.

It's my birthday.
I asked for money,
But Mom said, "That's
Not appropriate, honey!

"Dad and I are buying you
Some clothes for school."
I'd rather have
A swimming pool!

It's my birthday.
I asked for a puppy.
Aunt Sue sent a fish bowl
With a bright colored guppy!

It's my birthday.
I asked for a bike,
But nobody gets me
What I like.

Nobody listens
To what they're told.
This gift substitution
Is getting old!

A LITTLE CHILD SHALL LEAD THEM

In the towering western mountains
Hidden from the travelers' view
Lay in wait a band of Indians
To attack all who came through.

A wagon train moved across the prairie,
Led by wise old Colonel Bill.
Though this was the eve of Christmas,
It was not a night of *peace, goodwill!*

Many miles had come the settlers
Through dangers that would never cease.
Until they crossed the Indian country,
Only a miracle could bring peace.

But was not this the time for miracles,
This time of the Christ Child's birth?
But this band, blood-thirsty, savage,
Would not know the Christ Child's worth.

Such were thoughts of all the travelers
As the wagons jolted on.
Though they had not seen the Indians,
They had seen signs all along.

Not a sound did break the silence
Except the horses' steady plod.
Then came a sound—a distant wolf cry—
The travelers' fate was up to God.

All were waiting, tense and anxious,
Through the morning, through the day,
But still they did not see the Indians.
Shadows turned the prairie gray.

Then just as the sun was setting,
All eyes turned toward the spot
In the circle of the wagons
Where there stood an Indian tot!

Big dark eyes stared at the settlers.
Fear was written on his face.
Each one wondered how he'd come there,
How he wandered from his race.

Old Bill fed the boy his supper.
Strange tonight their paths had crossed…
Tonight a little child would lead them,
An Indian child, alone and lost.

An Indian lad, a wagon master
Started riding through the night.
Would a miracle be waiting?
Would a star guide them with light?

An Indian camp, a chief, his people—
Eyes that flickered with relief
When they saw the little boy,
Son of Red Cloud, Indian Chief.

Old Bill stood before the council,
Spoke of peace and waited there
Until Red Cloud finally answered,
"Go, for peace must start somewhere!"

Christmas morning, quiet and peaceful!
Not an Indian lurked about.
Wise men started on their journey.
The wagon train pulled slowly out.

The child to each a gift had given.
It was the best since Jesus' birth.
In the endless prairie country,
Peace had come once more to earth.

CHANGE

It was a blustery autumn day.
The trees were bare.
The sky was gray.
A hint of snow was in the air.
Leaves had fallen everywhere.
I wore my coat
When I went outside,
But the wind was biting
Into my hide.

I missed summer
With bright, sunny skies
And green, leafy branches
That shaded my eyes.
Change was so ugly!
Everything died!
I turned around
And went back inside.

A little while later
My dad called me out
Where great piles of leaves
Were all stacked about.
We rolled and we laughed
And we had so much fun,
I forgot how I missed
The warm summer sun.

This new warmth I felt
Came from within,
As we raked all the leaves
Into big piles again.

Then Dad and I
Went out to the fields
And gathered some pumpkins
For Thanksgiving meals.

Mom made apple cider
And hot, spicy pies.
She roasted a turkey
Of humongous size.
Then the doorbell rang
And I opened the door.
There were uncles and aunts
And cousins galore!

Then Grandma and Grandpa
Came carrying food
That put everyone
In a holiday mood.
Then from the gray sky
Came huge sparkling flakes
And brought us the magic
That wintertime makes.

WHAT I LIKE

I like colored kites
That soar in the wind,
And long country lanes
That frequently bend.

I like yellow puppies
With small, wagging tails,
And bubbling streams
Where my little boat sails.

I like to climb trees
And catch wooly worms,
And laugh at my sister
When she sees them and squirms.

People say someday
I'll soar on planes
And forget flying kites
And long country lanes.

I'll take yellow cabs
With taillights that blink,
And sail on big boats
And hope they don't sink.

I'll climb to the top
Of a big corporation,
And leave wooly worms
For a worse aggravation.

But people don't know
How much I enjoy
Each of my days
Just being a boy.

It would be rude to tell them,
But I wish they'd shut up!
I will grow older,
But I'll never grow up!

BEST FRIENDS

(Lonnie and Jerry)

One of the things my best friend likes
On a clear summer day, is riding our bikes.
We peddle like crazy and coast with hands free!
We race with the wind, my best friend and me!

We ride up dirt banks and jump narrow lanes,
We get cuts and scratches, but neither complains.
We take the back roads for a swim in the creek.
Then we're back on our bikes and off like a streak!

When we get older, we'll remember the thrill
Of riding our bikes over Russell Creek Hill.
I know we'll grow up and go separate ways,
But we'll always be friends from our bike-riding days.

When you finish this poem, I hope you'll go find
A very good friend, like that best friend of mine.
Then get on your bikes and ride off together.
It's a sure way to be best friends forever!

Printed in the United States
60515LVS00005B/529-576

9 781424 139408